Giants!

Giants!

STORIES FROM AROUND THE WORLD

PAUL ROBERT WALKER

Illustrated by James Bernardin

Harcourt Brace & Company

San Diego • New York • London

To Devin and Dariel, my little giants
—P. R. W.

To C. S. Lewis, N. C. Wyeth, and Mark Heard —
three giants in my eyes
—J. B.

Library of Congress Cataloging-in-Publication Data
Walker, Paul Robert.
Giants!: stories from around the world/[retold by] Paul Robert
Walker; illustrated by James Bernardin. — 1st ed.
p. cm.
Includes bibliographical references.
Contents: Jack and the beanstalk (England) — Kana the stretching wonder (Hawaii) — The giant who had no heart
(Norway) — The Cyclops (Ancient Greece) — The cannibal's wonderful bird (South Africa) —
Coyote and the giant sisters (Pacific Northwest) — David and Goliath (Ancient Israel)
ISBN 0-15-200883-7
1. Tales. 2. Giants — Folklore. [1. Giants — Folklore.
2. Folklore.] I. Bernardin, James, ill. II. Title.
PZ8.1.W1287Gi 1995
[398.2] — dc20   94-37086

First edition
A B C D E

Printed in Singapore

The illustrations in this book were done in gouache and Prismacolor pencil on BFK paper.
The title display was hand-lettered by Lloyd Kirkpatrick.
The text type was set in Cochin by PennSet, Inc.
Color separations by Bright Arts, Ltd., Singapore
Printed and bound by Tien Wah Press, Singapore
This book was printed with soya-based inks on Leykam recycled paper,
which contains more than 20 percent postconsumer waste and has
a total recycled content of at least 50 percent.
Production supervision by Warren Wallerstein and Kent MacElwee
Designed by Lisa Peters

Contents

Author's Note

LONG, LONG AGO, in the time before time, a race of giants walked upon the earth. Some were brave, high-minded heroes, but such great ones were unusual. Most giants were a greedy, dim-witted lot, hoarding treasure and living simple, solitary lives.

And then, not quite so long ago, a new race appeared on the earth — the human race. They were younger and smaller than the giants, and at first they were overmatched by the size and strength of the old ones. But the humans had something the giants lacked: a clever intelligence and special bravery that comes only with brains. Though there were ferocious battles, in time the humans defeated the giants and took over the earth.

Or so it was said, and so it was believed by people in many different cultures around the world. This tale is not told exactly as

I have told it by any particular people or in any particular story. But the basic idea — of an older race of giants and a conflict between giants and humans — lies behind the myths and folklore of cultures from every corner of the globe.

Why did people believe in giants? There are many reasons, but the most basic is the age-old attempt to understand the natural world. When primitive people gazed upon huge mountains in the hazy glow of twilight, they saw the homes of giants — or perhaps the mountains themselves seemed like sleeping giants ready to rise and stalk the earth. When the ground quaked and shook, it felt like the footsteps of giants. The rumble of thunder sounded like giants' laughter, while lakes or ponds might be giants' footprints filled with water. And when people looked up at the countless stars of the dark night, they saw giants arching across the sky.

There were other hints, as well, that pointed to the existence of giants. The bones of dinosaurs have lain in the earth for millions of years, but it was only in the nineteenth century that scientists identified them as belonging to prehistoric reptiles. What would a hunter think — perhaps ten thousand years ago — if he came upon the huge thighbone of *Tyrannosaurus rex?* It would be only natural to imagine that it belonged to a giant.

Of course, there have always been human beings who are taller than others, and long ago, when people lived in small groups, without modern means of travel or communication, these taller people seemed more unusual than they do today. Even now, when we can watch one seven-footer playing basketball against another seven-footer, there is still something fascinating about very tall people. I know, because I'm six-foot-six myself, and I've been called a giant more than once.

In researching this book, I had the pleasure of reading scores of wonderful stories from many different cultures. I've chosen seven of these stories to retell, reflecting a wide variety of folk traditions, from Europe and the Middle East to Africa, Hawaii, and the Pacific Northwest. Although I set out to represent the rich diversity of world folklore, my greatest concern was the quality of the stories themselves. These are all delightful tales, and I thoroughly enjoyed retelling them.

The original written versions of these stories vary, from the brilliant narrative poetry of Homer to the less polished oral tales recorded by folklorists. Regardless of literary quality, though, the original language and structure can be difficult and complex. So I've tried to retell the tales in a style that will appeal to young readers of today. While remaining true to the original spirit and main themes, I've combined ideas from different versions, changed details, and emphasized certain aspects of character and plot. Each story is followed by a brief nonfiction section that presents information about the original sources.

Of course, I can only provide the original *written* sources, and these tales were told long before they were written. They go deep into the shared memory of the human race, back into the long, long ago—the time before time, when giants walked the earth.

—P. R. W.

JACK AND THE BEANSTALK

England

O NCE UPON A TIME, a boy named Jack lived with his widowed mother in a tiny, run-down cottage. Jack and his mother were so poor that they barely had enough to eat — and Jack made them even poorer with his lazy habits and foolish ways.

Whenever they had a spare penny or something special for supper, Jack lost it or forgot it or gave it away. Instead of working, he sat around day after day doing next-to-nothing at all. Yet his mother loved him just the same, for he was all she had in the world — except for an old spotted milk cow.

One day, Jack's mother came to him with tears in her eyes. "Oh, Jack," she said, "we have no food or money left. You must go to town and sell our cow. I hate to part with her — she's been such a good cow — but if we don't sell her we'll starve."

For a moment, Jack felt sad about his mother's tears and his own foolishness. But he quickly forgot about it and led the cow toward town, whistling happily along the way. Jack was a sturdy fellow, and he enjoyed nothing more than a good outing.

On the road, he met the butcher. When Jack explained that he wanted to sell the cow, the butcher took off his rumpled hat and showed him five colored beans that he'd hidden in its crown.

"I'll trade you these beans for the cow," the butcher offered.

Jack gazed longingly at the beans in the butcher's hand. At that moment, he believed they were the most beautiful beans he'd ever seen. "Done!" said Jack.

And so the butcher went on to town, leading the spotted milk cow, while Jack walked back home with the five colored beans.

"Mother, Mother!" he cried. "Look what I've gotten for our cow!"

Jack was such a foolish boy that he thought his mother would be happy to see the five colored beans. But of course she wasn't happy at all; she was heartbroken. She grabbed the beans from his hand and threw them out into the yard. Then she sent him to bed without his supper, for there wasn't a crumb to eat in the house.

Early the next morning, Jack rose and crept out to the yard, hoping to find his five colored beans. But instead of the beans, he discovered five giant beanstalks winding and twining together like a ladder up to the sky! Jack scrambled onto the beanstalk, climbing higher and higher and higher, until he stepped out into a strange new world above the clouds.

Exhausted and hungry from his long climb, Jack walked all day

through the cloud-world, hoping to find a house where he might ask for something to eat. But there were no houses to be seen; no trees or animals or other living things—only uncut rocks and scattered piles of dark brown earth.

Out of nowhere, an old woman appeared in Jack's path. Wrinkles creased her sickly face, and tattered clothes hung upon her frail body. But despite her weak appearance, her voice was strong and commanding.

"What are you doing here, boy?" she asked.

When Jack explained about the five colored beans and the giant beanstalk ladder, the old woman asked him a strange, surprising question. "Do you remember your father?"

"No, ma'am," Jack replied. "And whenever I ask my mother about him, she starts to cry."

"Well, I will tell you what your mother cannot. You see, Jack, I was your father's fairy, so I knew him very well. He was the richest and best-hearted man in the whole county. An evil giant learned of your father's generosity and pretended to be a poor man who had lost everything in an earthquake. Your father took pity on him and invited the giant and his wife to live with your family. You were only a few months old.

"All the time he lived in your house, the giant looked for a chance to steal your father's riches. Then, one day when the servants were away, the cruel brute killed your father, stole his treasure, and burned your house to the ground."

Jack stared at the strange old woman. "I thought you were his fairy," he said. "Why didn't you save him?"

The old woman cast her eyes down in embarrassment. "Fairies must follow rules, just as humans do," she explained. "In a moment of foolishness, I broke the rules and lost my powers. I regained them only yesterday, as you were taking your cow to town. It was I who made you take the five colored beans, and I who made the beanstalk grow toward the sky. Now the rest is up to you."

"Up to me?" asked Jack. "What do you mean?"

"The giant who killed your father lives in this country. You must take the treasure that is yours and avenge the death of your father." With these words, the old wrinkled fairy disappeared into the clouds.

All that day, Jack walked through the strange new land, thinking about his father and the evil giant. His feet ached and his stomach grumbled with hunger, but he felt different and happy. For the first time in his life, he knew who he was.

Near sundown, he came to a large mansion with an open door. A plain-looking woman stood in the doorway, and Jack asked her if she might give him a bite to eat.

"I'd love to, dearie," said the woman. "After all, we don't get many travelers in these parts. But my husband is a ferocious giant who eats nothing but human flesh. In fact, he's out right now hunting for supper."

Jack's heart pounded at the woman's words, but the thought of his father—and the grumbling in his stomach—was even stronger than his fear. So he begged and pleaded until the giant's wife invited him into the mansion. They walked down a long, dark hallway past a wall of iron bars, and from behind the bars came the cries of the poor human victims waiting to be served on the giant's table.

In the kitchen, the plain woman gave Jack all he wanted to eat and drink—for she was a generous, kindhearted soul. But just as he finished his supper, a loud stomping rattled the walls of the mansion. *Stomp! Stomp! Stomp!*

"My husband!" the woman cried. "Quick, hide in the oven!" So Jack jumped into the oven while the giant's wife went to answer the door.

From his hiding place, Jack heard the thundering footsteps and booming voice of the giant. "I smell fresh meat!" he roared.

"Oh no, my dear," said his wife soothingly, "it's just the people in the dungeon."

"*Hmmph!*" snorted the giant, stepping loudly into the kitchen. Then, with two great strides, he walked casually toward the oven and bent down to peek at what was cooking inside—which sent Jack scrambling back behind a pie. But after a curious glance, the giant just turned away and shouted, "Bring me food!"

Peering over the pie, Jack watched the monster gulp down his evening meal and tried not to think about what—or whom—he was eating. When the giant was done, he got up from the table and went to sit by the fire.

"Bring me my hen!" he grunted.

A few moments later, the giant's wife appeared with a very pretty hen. Then she went off to bed, leaving the giant and the hen sitting by the fire.

"Lay!" ordered the giant. Jack's eyes grew wide with wonder as the hen laid a perfect golden egg at the giant's command. But that was only the beginning. Again and again the giant ordered the hen to lay, until he had a pile of golden eggs in his lap. Tired of the game, he fell asleep beside the fire, snoring like the roar of a cannon.

Carefully, Jack climbed out of the oven, seized the hen, and tiptoed down the long, dark hallway. Leaving the mansion behind, he ran through the world above the clouds until he came to the beanstalk. By the time he reached his own backyard, the sun was rising and his poor mother was beside herself with grief—for she feared he had come to a bad end through his own foolishness.

Jack assured his mother that he was just fine. Then he showed her the pretty hen and ordered it to lay. Sure enough, the hen produced a perfect egg of solid gold. "You see, Mother," said Jack, "I'm not so foolish after all. We will never be poor or hungry again."

Jack and his mother lived happily in their cottage, with the hen producing as many golden eggs as they desired. But in time Jack grew restless, thinking about the riches that the giant had stolen from his father. One morning, he rose early and rubbed a special plant on his face to darken his complexion. Then he put on a big, floppy hat and climbed the beanstalk to the world above the clouds.

When he reached the mansion, the giant's wife was once again standing in the doorway. Jack approached her and, disguising his voice, asked for something to eat and drink.

"I'd love to, dearie," she replied, "but I don't think so. You see, the last time I let a boy into our house, he stole my husband's magic hen. And the big brute has been in a terrible mood ever since. He's not in a very good mood to begin with, so—well, you can just imagine!"

Jack felt sorry for the giant's wife, but he begged and pleaded until the good-hearted woman led him to the kitchen. Just as he was finishing his supper, a loud stomping rattled the walls. *Stomp! Stomp! Stomp!*

"My husband! Quick, hide in the cupboard!" Jack scrambled into the cupboard while the giant's wife answered the door. Once again, he heard the thundering footsteps and booming voice of the giant.

"I smell fresh meat!"

"Oh no, my dear, it's only a piece of dead rabbit that the crows dropped down the chimney."

"*Hmmph!*" the giant snorted, stepping loudly into the kitchen. From the cupboard, Jack watched the monster plop down at the

11

table and eat his huge meal, just as he had before. But this time, after supper he ordered his wife to bring his money bags. The poor woman could barely drag them down the stairs, they were so full of gold and silver. For hours the giant counted his treasure, until he fell asleep beside the fire.

When the house shook with the monster's snores, Jack sneaked out of the cupboard, lifted the heavy bags over his shoulder, and escaped out into the world above the clouds. By the time he descended the beanstalk, the sun was rising and his mother was worried sick. Jack showed her the two huge bags of gold and silver, saying, "You see, Mother, now if anything happens to our hen, we will still be provided for."

His mother smiled and hugged him close. "You're a good boy, Jack. But I wish you would cut down this horrible beanstalk."

"I can't do that, Mother," Jack replied. "Not yet."

For a time, Jack tried to forget about the giant and the beanstalk, but the words of the old wrinkled fairy came back to him again and again: "You must take the treasure that is yours and avenge the death of your father." So one morning he colored his hair and put on a strange costume. Then he climbed the beanstalk and found his way to the giant's mansion.

Once again, the giant's wife was standing in the doorway, and once again Jack convinced her to let him into the kitchen. When the giant returned with a *Stomp! Stomp! Stomp!* Jack hopped into a copper kettle.

"I smell fresh meat!" the giant roared.

"Oh no, my dear," his wife began, "it is . . ."

"No excuses! I smell fresh meat in this kitchen, and I will find

12

it!" Jack's heart raced with terror as the giant searched every nook and cranny of the kitchen. When the monster placed his huge hand on the lid of the copper kettle, the boy held his breath and waited for death. But the brute just shook the kettle a bit and moved it out of the way, with Jack safe and alive inside.

Satisfied that there was no fresh meat in the kitchen, the giant ate an enormous dinner, washed down with glass after glass of foaming ale. When he was done, he plopped beside the fire and called to his wife, "Bring me my harp."

A moment later, the giant's wife appeared carrying the most beautiful harp Jack had ever seen. She set the instrument on the table, and the giant grunted, "Play!" Immediately, the harp began to play lovely, magical music all by itself.

Of all the giant's treasures, Jack thought this was the greatest, and he wanted it more than he had ever wanted a thing in his life. It wasn't long before the soothing music of the harp lulled the giant into a deep sleep. Carefully, quietly, Jack climbed out of the copper kettle, tiptoed across the room, and grabbed the harp in his hands.

"Master! Master!" cried the harp. "A thief!"

Roused by the cries of the harp, the giant lumbered to his huge feet and followed Jack out of the kitchen. "I'll get you, boy!" he bellowed. "And eat you for dessert!"

Clutching the magic harp, Jack bolted out the door and raced through the world above the clouds. The giant closed in behind him, his long, powerful legs leaping the uncut rocks and dark brown piles of earth. But just when the boy felt the monster's breath on his neck, the big oaf fell behind—too sleepy and full of food and drink. Jack gripped the beanstalk and scrambled down, with the giant still lumbering after him.

When Jack landed in his own backyard, he found his mother waiting for him with tears streaming down her face, afraid that this time he had met a bad end for sure.

"Quick, Mother!" he shouted. "Bring me the ax!"

The startled woman ran straight for the cottage and brought the ax just as the giant descended through the clouds. Jack chopped down the beanstalk with five strong blows, one for each of the five colored beans. Like a mountain falling to earth, the giant tumbled and landed with a horrible crash in Jack's backyard—as dead as dead can be.

At that moment, the wrinkled old fairy appeared and the magic harp began to play a beautiful song it had once played for Jack's father. As the fairy explained all that had happened, Jack put his arm around his mother and comforted her for the sadness of the past. "No one can bring back Father," he said, "but at least we can live happily now."

And so they did—happily ever after.

This story is based on the earliest written version of "Jack and the Beanstalk," published in 1807 by English bookseller Benjamin Tabart and edited by the philosopher William Godwin. Almost all twentieth-century retellings of the story are based on a somewhat different version told by Joseph Jacobs, first published in 1890 in English Fairy Tales.

The major difference between the two versions is that Jacobs did not include the fairy who tells Jack how the giant killed his father and stole his riches. He believed that the fairy was added to the original oral tale in order to give Jack a "good" reason for stealing the giant's treasures. This is probably true; however, the fairy brings an interesting and different aspect to the story, so I decided to include her.

Another difference is that the giant in Jacobs' version says, "Fe-fi-fo-fum, I smell the blood of an Englishman," whereas the giant in the earlier version says, "I smell fresh meat!" "Fe-fi-fo-fum" is a standard formula in many English tales, but "fresh meat" seems more to the point.

On one level, "Jack and the Beanstalk" is the story of a rather foolish boy who finds wealth and happiness through his bravery and sense of adventure. On a deeper level, however, it reflects an idea found in many cultures throughout the world: the dream of climbing a ladder to the sky.

KANA THE STRETCHING WONDER

Hawaii

L ONG AGO on the island of Hawaii, a chief named Haka-lani-leo married a beautiful princess named Hina. Many other chiefs also wanted her for a wife, but Haka-lani-leo and Hina were happy together, and in time they had twelve sons.

The first ten sons were towering giants with bulging muscles. The eleventh son, Niheu, was much smaller than the others — almost a dwarf. Yet he proved stronger and more clever than all the rest combined. But the twelfth son, Kana, was born in the form of a rope — nothing but a long piece of rope! He didn't look like a son at all, so Haka-lani-leo and Hina tossed him into the pigpen.

Fortunately, the rope-baby had a wise old grandmother named Uli, who knew much about the ways and wonders of the world. She rescued Kana from the pigpen and carried him to her own house in the mountains high above the village. There she placed him in a calabash full of water. Immediately he began to change, and in four days the rope became a child.

But that was only the beginning of the wonder. The child grew and grew, until in forty days he was forty feet long, with big, round eyes as bright as the moon. Then Kana grew longer and longer still, until he could not even fit in Uli's house. So she lengthened her house to fit her growing grandson, until finally Kana — and Uli's house — stretched from the mountains to the sea!

In the meantime, Kana's parents forgot about the piece of rope they had tossed into the pigpen. One morning, his mother, the beautiful Hina, went out surfing near the village. As she rode the curling waves, she noticed a strange, palm-covered hill floating in the open water beyond a coral reef. Curious, she paddled over the reef and climbed onto the hill, walking in the cool shade of the waving palms. Suddenly, magically, the hill floated away, taking Hina across the sea.

When Haka-lani-leo discovered his wife missing, he asked his sons for help. But, although the ten giant brothers were very strong, they were not very smart. Only clever Niheu could solve the mystery. "Father," he said, "our mother has been kidnapped by the chief of Molokai. He has carried her away on his floating hill, the one they call Haupu."

"What shall we do?" asked Haka-lani-leo. "Can you rescue her?"

Niheu gazed down at the sand. "No, Father, I cannot. For my strength is greatest on the island of Hawaii. On Molokai I might be too weak to fight the chief's magic."

Just then, Kana appeared on the beach, his head and shoulders stretching up toward the tropical sky. Out in the surf, the ten giant brothers were fighting over a huge fish. Niheu and his father watched in amazement as Kana stepped out into the sparkling water and took the fish away from the giants as easily as if they were children playing with a toy.

"Who are you?" asked Haka-lani-leo.

"I am Kana, the one you threw in the pigpen." As he spoke, Kana's moon eyes flashed so brightly that his father turned away and ran back toward the safety of the village. But Niheu stood his ground and looked up at his younger brother.

"Our mother has been kidnapped by the chief of Molokai," he explained. "He has powerful magic, but I see you have powerful magic, too. Will you help me rescue her?"

Kana thought for a moment. "She did not treat me well," he said, "but still she is my mother. Yes, I will help you."

When Niheu told his father of the rescue mission, Haka-lani-leo ordered his men to carve a double war canoe big enough to hold Kana. The men of the village worked for many days, until they had finished the biggest canoe that had ever been seen on the island. But when Kana stepped out into the water and began to get into the boat, the weight of his hand sunk the canoe beneath the waves.

Haka-lani-leo ordered his men to carve another canoe, even bigger than the first. But again, the weight of Kana's hand sunk the canoe beneath the waves. Finally, Kana's grandmother, Uli, came down from the mountains to help them. "You must go to the hills of Paliuli," she told them, "and dig up the great canoe called Kau-mai-eliel."

19

The men of the ocean village thought it very strange to go up into the hills and dig for a canoe. But they obeyed Uli and dug in the hills of Paliuli. They worked all day in the warm rain and the hot sun, in the angry thunder and the flashing lightning, until they uncovered the giant war canoe and dragged it down to the sea.

This time Kana got into the canoe without sinking it, but he was so tall that he had to fold himself up to fit inside. Niheu climbed in after him, and together the brothers paddled off across the deep, blue water to rescue their mother.

Near the island of Molokai, the chief held Hina captive in a thatched house high atop his floating hill. Knowing that her sons would try to rescue her, he sent his two messenger birds, Plover and Snipe, out over the sea to search for signs of a war party. When the birds returned and told him of the giant war canoe, the chief sent out his greatest warrior — the Swordfish.

Out in the open sea, where the water is dark as indigo, the warrior Swordfish attacked the giant canoe, ramming its side with his long, sharp bill. Kana was unable to fight, because he was all folded up in the bottom of the boat. But Niheu raised his war club and smashed the Swordfish with a single powerful blow, sending him down to the depths of the ocean.

After his battle with the Swordfish, Niheu felt strong and eager for glory. When they reached Molokai, he didn't wait for Kana to unfold himself from the bottom of the canoe. Instead, he raced up the floating hill with his war club in his hand and smashed through a wall of thick green leaves protecting the house. Then he rushed inside and rescued his mother from the warriors of the chief.

As he carried her down the hill, Hina exclaimed, "Oh, Niheu, my son, though you are small, you are so strong and brave. And to think that the secret of your strength is in your hair!"

Circling overhead, the messenger birds, Plover and Snipe, heard the words of Hina and dove down to pull out Niheu's hair. As he raised his arms to defend himself, he dropped his mother, and Hina ran back to the house in fear. The birds tore five sacred hairs from the head of Niheu, and his great strength dwindled to nothing. Now it was up to Kana.

On the beach below, he unfolded himself from the war canoe and rose to his full height, stretching upward into the sky. But as Kana stretched to reach the house of the Molokai chief, the floating hill—Haupu—stretched with him, growing higher and higher and higher still. Kana stretched again, but again the hill stretched with him. Again and again and again.

Finally Kana stretched so high that his body grew thin as a spider web. Desperate for strength, he stretched back across the sea, over the island of Maui and the smoldering volcano of Haleakala, and across the sea again until he reached the house of Uli, high in the mountains of Hawaii. "Oh, Grandmother," he whispered, "I am so weak and thin. I cannot stretch any more."

"Don't worry, my grandson," said Uli, placing good food before him. "I will fatten you up."

As Kana ate the food prepared by Uli, strength and power flowed into his body. Back on Molokai, Niheu watched his brother's legs grow fatter and fatter. Finally, he grew tired of waiting and hacked at Kana's legs with a sharp stone ax.

"I feel pain," Kana told his grandmother.

"It is Niheu," Uli explained, "reminding you of your task."

21

GIANTS!

"But what shall I do?" asked Kana. "No matter how high I stretch, the floating hill stretches higher."

"Listen, Kana," Uli counseled. "The floating hill is a great turtle, and its power is in its flippers. You must reach into the sea and break the flippers from its body. Then it will stretch no more."

Kana raised himself up from Uli's house, arching back over the glistening ocean to the island of Molokai. With the good food in his belly, Kana stretched high above the turtle-hill and reached down into the warm water to break off the flipper on the right side. Then he stretched back over the hill, reached down into the water, and broke off the flipper on the left side.

Without its flippers, the great turtle collapsed to its normal size. Kana lifted his mother out of the chief's house and gently placed her in the war canoe. Then he picked up his brother Niheu and placed him beside her. Finally, he raised his huge leg and stepped on the back of the great turtle, smashing it to tiny pieces, which became the turtles that still swim in the waters of Hawaii.

When Kana and Niheu returned with the beautiful Hina, the whole village welcomed them with feasting, singing, and dancing. But though Kana joined the celebration, he did not stay and live with his family. Instead, he went up to the long house of his grandmother, Uli, where he could stretch his great body from the mountains to the sea.

The oral literature of Hawaii is rich with stories ranging from myths of gods and goddesses to tales of historical chiefs and heroes. The legends of Kana and Niheu—part human, part divine—fall between the myths of

gods and the stories of men. This type of hero, called a kupua, appears in many Hawaiian legends.

A kupua hero may be a shape shifter, like Kana, or he may demonstrate extraordinary strength or power with a war club, like Niheu. The great turtle-hill, Haupu, is a kupua in animal form, and the struggle between rival kupua is typical of many stories. The idea that the grandmother saves the kupua when he is born in nonhuman form is also a common element.

There are a number of legends featuring Kana and Niheu. The story of how they rescued their mother was written down in several versions, beginning in the second half of the nineteenth century. All are quite similar, and I have combined details from different versions to create this story. Although the Kana legend refers to many specific places in the Hawaiian Islands, similar legends are found throughout the islands of the South Pacific.

THE GIANT WHO HAD
NO HEART

Norway

ONCE THERE WAS a king who had seven sons and loved them with all his heart.

He loved them so deeply that he never allowed all seven out of his sight at the same time, but always kept one close beside him. So when it came time for them to marry, the king sent his six oldest sons out into the world, wearing the finest clothes his treasure could buy and riding the finest horses in his kingdom. But he kept his youngest son, whose name was Boots, at home in the castle and told the others to bring back a princess for Boots.

The six princes traveled throughout the world, visiting kings and kingdoms until they found a king with six beautiful daughters. After gentle words and wooing, the brothers won the hearts of the princesses and set off for home in a royal procession that dazzled the eyes of all who saw it. But the six brothers completely forgot about finding a princess for Boots.

Now it happened that the royal procession passed a steep mountain, where the castle of a terrible giant perched on the highest peak. As soon as the giant saw the princes and princesses riding beneath him, he turned them all into stone.

Meanwhile, the king waited and waited for the return of his six sons. Each day his heart grew sadder, until finally his youngest son, Boots, offered to go and search for his brothers.

"Oh no!" the king exclaimed. "You must never leave me, for without you I would have no reason to live."

But Boots had his heart set on adventure, and he begged and pleaded until his kindhearted father let him go. The king had given the six oldest brothers all his best horses and spent his treasure on their fine clothing, so he had nothing left for Boots except an old broken-down nag. That didn't bother Boots; he cheerfully put on his worn-out clothes and mounted the old nag.

"Good-bye, Father," he said. "I shall return sure enough, and who knows — I might bring my brothers home as well."

After riding for some time, Boots came upon a raven lying in the middle of the road, weakly flapping its wings. "Please!" cried the raven. "I am so hungry that I can't even fly. Give me some of your food, and I will help you when you need it most."

Boots got off his horse and bent over the raven. "I don't have much food," he said, "and you don't look like you could be much help to me. But I will gladly share what food I have, since you need it so badly." Boots gave the raven some of his food, until the bird felt strong enough to fly away.

After riding farther, the young prince came to a stream with a big salmon lying on the shore, thrashing and wiggling on the rocks. "Please!" cried the salmon. "Push me back into the water, and I will help you when you need it most."

Boots got off his horse and bent over the salmon. "You don't look like you could be much help to me," he said. "But I will gladly help you back into the water." So he pushed the salmon into the stream and watched it swim away.

Boots rode farther and farther still, until he came upon a wolf, dragging itself desperately along the edge of the road. "Please!" cried the wolf. "I am so hungry that I can hear the wind whistling through my stomach. Give me your horse to eat."

Boots got off his horse and stood above the hungry wolf. "This is ridiculous," he said. "First, I came to a raven and gave him my food. Then I came to a salmon and pushed him back into the stream. And now you want my horse—but then I would have nothing to ride on."

"You can ride on me," promised the wolf, "and I will help you when you need it most."

"You don't look like you could be much help to me," Boots replied, "but since you are so hungry, you may have my horse." So the wolf ate the old nag, until he was strong and healthy again. Boots put the bit of the bridle in the wolf's mouth and laid the saddle across its gray back. Then he mounted the wolf and rode off faster than he had ever ridden before.

After a time, the boy and wolf came to a steep mountain with a castle perched on its highest peak. "This is the land of a terrible giant," the wolf explained, "and over there you can see your six brothers and their six brides, whom the giant has turned to stone. Way up on top of the mountain is the door of the giant's castle, and in that door you must go."

Boots gazed up at the door and shook his head. "The giant will kill me for sure."

"Not at all," the wolf replied. "Inside the castle you will meet a princess. She will tell you how to put an end to the giant."

So Boots climbed the mountain and entered the door of the castle. Sure enough, he found a princess waiting inside, just as the wolf had said he would. And what a princess she was! Boots thought she was the most beautiful girl he had ever seen.

"Good heavens!" the princess exclaimed when she saw Boots. "What brings you here? It will surely be your death; no one can kill the giant who lives in this castle, for he has no heart in his body."

Boots explained that he had come to rescue his six brothers, who were turned to stone outside. "And as long as I'm here," he declared, "I'll rescue you as well."

"Well, since you're here—and so handsome, too," the princess added, "we'll do the best we can. Quick, hide under the bed! I hear the giant coming."

No sooner had Boots slipped under the bed than the giant entered the huge door of the castle. "I smell human blood!" he shouted.

"Don't worry, dear," the princess soothed. "It's just a magpie who dropped a man's bone down the chimney. I threw it out right away, but the smell stays longer than the bone."

The giant grunted and said no more about it. That night, as he lay down upon his big bed, the princess asked, "Tell me, dear, where do you keep your heart? I've always wondered, since you don't keep it with your body."

"You don't need to worry about that," said the giant. "But since you ask, it's under the stone slab at the front of the door."

Hiding under the bed, Boots thought to himself, *Ah! So that's where it is. We'll soon take care of that!*

The next morning, as soon as the giant went off into the woods, Boots and the princess lifted the stone slab and looked for the giant's heart. Though they dug deeply, they found nothing but earth.

"He's made a fool of me this time," the princess admitted, "but I'll ask him again." So Boots put back the door slab, and the princess decorated it with the most beautiful flowers she could find. That evening when the giant came home, Boots hid under the bed again.

"I smell human blood!" the giant bellowed.

"I'm sorry, dear," said the princess. "It's just another magpie that dropped a man's bone down the chimney. I got rid of it as fast as I could."

The giant grunted and asked, "Who put all those flowers in the doorway?"

"Why, I did, of course. Since that is where you keep your heart, I wanted to make it beautiful."

The giant chuckled out loud. "What a foolish girl you are. It isn't there at all."

"Where is it then?" asked the princess.

The giant pointed across the room. "It's there, in the cupboard."

Hiding under the bed, Boots thought to himself, *Ah! So that's where it is. We'll soon take care of that!*

The next morning, when the giant went out into the woods, Boots and the princess searched the cupboard. They moved every dish, every cup, and every saucer, but they found no trace of the giant's heart.

"He's fooled me again," sighed the princess. "We must try once more." She decorated the cupboard with the most beautiful flowers she could find, and that evening when the giant came home, Boots hid under the bed once again.

"I smell human blood!" roared the giant.

"I know, dear," replied the princess. "It's that pesky magpie again. It dropped a man's bone down the chimney, and I just this moment threw it out."

The giant grunted and said no more about it. "Who put those silly flowers around the cupboard?" he asked.

"Why, I did, of course. Since that is where you keep your heart, I wanted to make it beautiful."

The giant laughed out loud. "You really are a foolish girl to believe such a story."

"How could I help but believe it," asked the princess, "since that is what you told me? After all, you know how fond I am of you, and it means so much to me to be close to your heart."

The giant plopped down on the big bed and pulled off his huge boots. "You can never be close to my heart," he said. "For my heart is in a place you can never go. Far, far away lies an island in a lake. On that island stands a church, and in that church is a well. In that well swims a duck, and in that duck grows an egg. And in that egg is my heart."

Hiding under the bed, Boots heard the giant's words and thought

to himself, *Ah! So that's where he keeps his heart! But how will I ever find it?*

Early the next morning, when the giant went off to the woods, Boots said good-bye to the princess and climbed down the steep hill. He found the wolf waiting for him beside the road and explained all that had happened inside the giant's castle. The wolf told Boots to jump on its back, and they ran off as swiftly as the wind, over hills and mountains, until at last they came to the lake with an island in the middle.

"How will we ever cross?" asked Boots. "The water looks cold and deep and treacherous."

"Don't worry," the wolf assured him, "just hold on tight, and I

31

will swim across." The wolf carried Boots through the cold water to the island, where they found the church easily enough. But the key hung on a hook so high that only the giant could reach it.

"Call the raven," suggested the wolf.

Boots called, and in the blink of an eye the raven appeared, grasped the key in its beak, and carried it down to him. "Thank you for your kindness," said the raven as it flew off into the sky.

Inside the church, Boots found the well with the duck swimming at the bottom, just as the giant had described. He hung over the top of the well and called to the duck, coaxing her with kind words and gentle sounds. Finally, the duck flew up and into his hands. But just as he caught her, she laid the egg, and it dropped down into the well.

"Call the salmon," said the wolf.

Boots called, and in the blink of an eye the salmon appeared, dove down into the well, and returned with the egg in its mouth. "Thank you for your kindness," said the salmon as it flopped back into the water.

"Squeeze the egg," the wolf advised.

Boots squeezed, and the painful scream of the giant carried across the hills and mountains to the well inside the church.

"Squeeze it again," counseled the wolf.

Again Boots squeezed the egg, and again the giant's scream carried into the church. "Please!" he bellowed. "I will do anything you ask. Anything at all."

"Bring my six brothers back to life," Boots commanded. "And their six brides as well."

"Yes, of course," moaned the giant. "I will do it this instant."

THE GIANT WHO HAD NO HEART

"Now destroy the egg," the wolf ordered.

Boots crushed the egg in his hand, and at that moment the terrible giant shattered into a thousand pieces.

When he returned to the giant's castle, Boots found his six brothers and their six brides alive and well on the side of the mountain. He climbed the steep slope and escorted his own princess out of the castle. Then the whole royal procession journeyed homeward, with Boots and his princess riding ahead on the back of the wolf.

The king was overjoyed to see his seven sons again, each with a beautiful princess as his bride. "But the most beautiful is the bride of Boots," the king declared, "and he shall sit at the head of the table with her."

In no time at all, the princes and princesses were married, and the king gave a great wedding feast that lasted for many days — so many days, in fact, that some believe they're still feasting this very minute.

This story was collected by Norwegian folklorists Peter Christen Asbjörnsen and Jorgen Möe during the first half of the nineteenth century. Asbjörnsen and Möe were childhood friends who began collecting folktales while working as tutors in rural Norway. Later, Asbjörnsen became a naturalist, and often traveled throughout the country accompanied by Möe, who became a respected poet. They continued to coax stories out of people they met, and they published them in a series of books, beginning in 1841 with Norwegian Folktales.

The idea of a giant who has no heart in his body is found in stories throughout Europe and Asia. In my own research for this book, I came across four different versions of the story: two from Ireland, one from Lapland, and another from Scandinavia. Readers will also note some similarities with "Jack and the Beanstalk," for in both stories the giant smells the blood of the human intruder and the young man is hidden by the lady of the giant's house.

The youngest son who ends up doing all the work is the hero of many Norwegian folktales—sort of a male version of Cinderella. In Norwegian, he is usually called Askeleden, but I've decided to use the name Boots from the English translation by G. W. Dasent.

THE CYCLOPS

Ancient Greece

ODYSSEUS CLUTCHED the rail of his ship and stared into the wind. His weathered, cunning eyes searched the horizon for a sign of land — a rock, an island, anything. But there was only storm-tossed, foaming sea.

For ten long years, Odysseus and his men had been away from home, fighting in the Trojan War. Now they were sailing back to Greece, anxious to see their loved ones again. Day after day they rode the waves, blown off course by angry winds, their food and water dwindling to nothing.

Then late one night, in the blackness without a moon, the Greeks found a calm harbor at the edge of the stormy sea. As if guided by a friendly god, they sailed safely through the dark water until their ship ran aground on a sandy beach.

The next morning, in the rosy light of dawn, Odysseus gazed at the rocky, mountainous land that loomed above the beach. "I wonder what kind of people live here," he said to his crew. "Are they savage and violent, or are they civilized and generous to strangers? I'll take a dozen men to find out. The rest of you stay and guard the ship."

Taking food for their journey and a goatskin full of pure black wine, Odysseus and his companions climbed the steep path that led up from the beach. Not far from the water, they came upon an enormous cave with rocky walls reaching up into the heart of the mountain. Inside they discovered wooden pens full of kids and lambs, clay jars overflowing with milk, and woven baskets packed with cheeses.

Odysseus' men begged him to take some of the food and head back to the safety of their ship. But Odysseus refused. "I want to see what kind of man lives in this great cave," he explained. "He must be a herdsman, out with his goats and sheep. Perhaps he will be generous to strangers who have lost their way." So the Greeks helped themselves to the cheeses and waited for the herdsman to return.

That evening, a monstrous creature filled the mouth of the cave and threw a load of firewood onto the floor with a crash that sent the Greeks scurrying to the darkest corner. The giant herdsman led his sheep and goats into the cavern and sealed the entrance with a boulder as big as a mountaintop. Then he lit his fire and began to milk his flocks, guiding the kids and lambs to their mothers as he finished.

From their hiding place, the Greeks gazed in wonder at their host, illuminated by the flickering light of the flames. He was a Cyclops—a towering brute with a single eye in the middle of his forehead. But though he looked like a hideous monster, he milked his sheep and goats with a gentle touch. *Perhaps he is civilized after all*, thought Odysseus.

When the Cyclops finished his chores, he noticed the tiny Greeks in the corner of the cave. "Who are you?" he asked, his voice rumbling against the rocky walls. "Are you pirates who come to steal from a stranger?"

Odysseus stepped forward. Dwarfed by the giant Cyclops, he stood strong and straight, his noble head held high. "We are Greeks returning from Troy," he explained. "We have been blown off course by the winds, and now we are at your mercy. In our land, we are always generous to strangers, for this is the will of Zeus. We hope that you will be generous, too."

The Cyclops laughed at Odysseus. "You are a simple fool," he said. "I have no fear of Zeus, for I am a son of the great god Poseidon, Lord of the Sea. I am Polyphemus, and I did not invite you to my cave."

Suddenly the Cyclops grabbed two of Odysseus' men in his powerful hands and smashed their skulls against the hard ground. Then he roasted them over his fire and ate them for dinner, washed down with foaming jars of milk. When he was full, the Cyclops fell asleep among his goats and sheep.

Outraged, Odysseus drew his sword and approached the sleeping giant. But as he climbed onto the monster's chest, he realized that only the Cyclops was strong enough to move the boulder that sealed the entrance of the cave. If he killed the one-eyed brute, the

Greeks would never escape. So Odysseus put away his sword and began to form a plan.

The next morning, the Cyclops lit his fire and milked his well-fed flocks. Then he grabbed two more of Odysseus' men, smashed their brains out, and ate them for breakfast. When he was finished, he rolled the boulder from the mouth of the cave as easily as if it were a pebble. Guarding the stone doorway, he led his flock out into the daylight and rolled the boulder back into place, locking the Greeks in gloomy darkness.

As soon as the monster was gone, Odysseus sprang into action. The Cyclops had left a fresh-cut olive tree to dry, so he could use it as a walking stick. Odysseus cut off the top of the tree — a pole taller than a man — and his companions smoothed it and sharpened it to a point. Then they held the tip over the fire until the wood was hard. When it was ready, they hid the sharp pole in the corner of the cave.

That evening, the Cyclops again led his flocks into the cavern and sealed the entrance with the huge boulder. He lit his fire, milked his sheep and goats, and guided the lambs and kids to their mothers. When his chores were done, he grabbed two more of Odysseus' men, smashed their brains out, and roasted them over the flames for dinner.

As the Cyclops began to wash down his horrible meal with milk, Odysseus stepped forward with a bowl of the black wine he had carried from the ship. "Here, Cyclops," he said pleasantly, "have a drink of this instead. It is like no other wine in the world, made of nectar and ambrosia. I would have offered it earlier, but you were too busy eating my friends."

GIANTS!

The Cyclops took the wine and drained the bowl in a single gulp. He handed it back to Odysseus and asked for more. And more again. When he had drunk three bowls of the pure black wine, he became more friendly. "Tell me, stranger," he asked, "what is your name? This wine has pleased me so much that I wish to give you a gift in return."

Odysseus thought quickly and answered, "You ask my name and I will tell you truly, but you must give me the gift you promised. My name is Nobody."

"Well, Nobody," said the Cyclops, chuckling crudely at his cruel joke, "here is my gift to you. I will eat you last, after I eat the rest of your friends." As soon as the words were out of his mouth, the monster slumped to the floor of the cave and fell into a deep, drunken sleep, with wine and bits of men dribbling out of his mouth.

While the snores of the Cyclops rattled the rocky walls, Odysseus held the sharp pole in the embers of the fire, heating the point until it glowed. Then he lifted the weapon in his muscular arms and, along with his men, climbed onto the giant face of the sleeping Cyclops. With a mighty shove, they drove the red-hot point into the eye of the monster.

"My eye!" he roared. "I am blind!"

The Greeks scrambled away as the Cyclops sat up and pulled the sharp pole out of his eye. "Neighbors!" he screamed. "Come and help me! I've been attacked by strangers! I've been blinded!"

Outside the cave, the other Cyclopians gathered. "What's wrong, Polyphemus?" they asked. "Who has injured you?"

"Nobody!" shouted Polyphemus. "Nobody has done this to me!"

"Well, if nobody did it to you," the others replied, "then you

40

must be having a bad dream. Go back to sleep. And stop disturbing the neighborhood." With that, the other Cyclopians returned to their caves.

When his neighbors were gone, Polyphemus felt his way to the mouth of the cave and rolled away the great boulder. He sat in the entrance, ready to catch anyone foolish enough to run past him. But Odysseus was too clever for such a simple trick. He gathered three woolly rams and tied them together with willow branches from the Cyclops' bed. He tied one of his men under the middle ram and did the same for each of his other men. Then he slipped under the belly of the biggest ram and held on tightly to the thick wool.

When the rosy dawn filled the mouth of the cave, the rams began to walk out toward the fields, just as they did each day. As the animals passed him, Polyphemus felt their backs, but in his blind agony he never guessed that the Greeks were tied beneath them. Finally, the biggest ram stood beside his master, with Odysseus clutching the wool beneath its belly.

"My dear old ram," said Polyphemus sadly, "why do you linger behind the others? You are usually the first to the fields, the first across the rivers, the first to return in the evening. Do you stay behind because you feel sorry for your poor blind master? If only you could speak like I do. Then you could tell me where that wicked Nobody is hiding."

But the ram could only bleat in reply, so he carried Odysseus past the Cyclops and out of the cave.

When they were a safe distance away, Odysseus slipped from beneath the ram and untied his companions. Then they led the fat sheep and goats down to the water's edge, loaded them onto the ship, and sailed out into the harbor.

When they were just the distance that a man's voice could still carry, Odysseus shouted across the water. "Cyclops! You ignored the will of Zeus and ate the guests in your own house. But now you see how great-hearted men and the power of the gods have punished you."

In a fury, the Cyclops broke off the tip of a mountain and hurled it out to sea. The mountaintop landed in front of Odysseus' ship, exploding water into the sky and driving the ship back toward shore. Desperately the Greeks rowed against the powerful wave, pulling away just beyond the Cyclops' grasp.

On the tiny ship, Odysseus still raged at the deaths of his companions. Although his men begged him not to stir the monster again, he could not resist his own angry heart. "Cyclops!" he shouted. "If any mortal man asks who blinded you, tell him it was Odysseus, the King of Ithaka!"

Standing alone on the shore, the blind Cyclops cried out to the god of the sea. "Father Poseidon, if I am truly your son, grant that Odysseus, the King of Ithaka, will never reach his home. Or if he must see his family again, then make him return alone, without his companions or his ship, and find troubles in his own household."

Again the monster broke off a mountaintop and hurled it at the Greek ship. But this time the huge boulder fell short, and the wave drove the ship forward, out through the calm harbor and into the storm-tossed, foaming sea. With the fat flocks of the Cyclops in their hold, the Greeks set sail for home, hoping to see their loved ones again.

Yet Poseidon had other plans, for the Lord of the Sea had heard the prayer of his son, Polyphemus. Of all the men aboard the ship, only Odysseus would reach his home. He would arrive as a beggar—after ten more years of wandering—to find terrible troubles in his own household.

But that is another story.

The story of Odysseus and the Cyclops is told in the Odyssey, *an epic poem composed around the eighth century* B.C. *An epic poem is a long "story" poem with many chapters (called "books"), similar in some ways to a modern novel. Most scholars believe that the* Odyssey *was composed by Homer, the great Greek poet who also composed the* Iliad, *an epic poem about the Trojan War. In Homer's time, poets sang their stories for the audience while accompanying themselves on a stringed instrument similar to a simple harp.*

No one knows if there really was a Greek king named Odysseus. But archaeologists have discovered evidence that the Greeks and Trojans did fight a war over the city of Troy sometime around the thirteenth or fourteenth century B.C. *The* Odyssey *tells the story of Odysseus' wanderings on the way back from the war and his homecoming in Ithaka. The adventure with the Cyclops is told in Book IX.*

Cyclops (or Kyklops) is a Greek word meaning "round-eyed" or "wheel-eyed." Many other cultures tell stories similar to the tale of Odysseus and the Cyclops. It's possible that these stories are based on Homer's story. But it's more probable that Homer himself based his story on an earlier folktale that passed from culture to culture.

43

Tales of one-eyed giants may have begun with the skull of an elephant, mammoth, or mastodon. The skulls of these animals have a large, round hole in the center where the trunk is attached to the head, while the real eye sockets are set to the side. If a person who had never seen a live specimen of the animal found such a skull, it would be natural to imagine that it belonged to a one-eyed giant.

THE CANNIBAL'S WONDERFUL BIRD

South Africa

ONE MORNING, in a distant African village, a group of girls went out into the bush to gather red clay. Among them was the daughter of the chief—a spirited young lady blessed with a beautiful singing voice.

While her friends scooped the clay into their baskets, the chief's daughter stood guard with a sharp-tipped spear, ready to protect them from lions and other wild creatures of the bush. But no wild animals came that day, and when their baskets were full the girls started back toward the village.

By this time the sun glared high in the sky, so the chief's daughter suggested that they visit a cool pond hidden among the trees. Leaving their clothes and jewelry on the shore, the girls dived into the refreshing water and played for hours, laughing and splashing and swimming. When they finally got out, the sun was sinking in the western sky.

Dressing quickly, the girls rushed back through the trees to the path. They were eager to reach their village before dark, for no one wants to be out in the bush at night. But when they were halfway home, the chief's daughter realized that she had left her golden earrings on the shore of the pond.

"They were a gift from my grandmother," she said sadly. "I must go back and get them. Who will go with me?"

She looked at each of her friends, one by one, but none of them offered to accompany her back to the pond. When she saw that they were afraid, the chief's daughter lifted her spear high above her head and thrust it angrily into the ground.

"If you won't go with me," she said in disgust, "you must stay here and watch the spear. If it falls to the ground, it means I have stumbled and fallen. If it stands up again, it means I'm all right. But if it stays on the ground, it means I'm dead." With that, the high-spirited girl walked back through the bush.

The others waited fearfully as dark shadows settled around them and unknown noises echoed across the bush. Suddenly the spear fell to the ground, and the girls shrieked with fright, "She's dead! Let's go!" They were so afraid that they ran back toward the village without waiting to see the spear spring up from the ground.

Out in the bush, the chief's daughter brushed herself off and continued on her way. It was nothing really, just a stumble along the path. But as she approached the pond, the sun sank in the western sky and darkness descended over the bush. Strange, frightening shapes and weird, eerie sounds echoed in the night. To keep up her courage, she began to sing in her clear, beautiful voice.

Now it happened that a giant cannibal was waiting at the

pond — a horrible creature with an ugly face and one huge foot. When he heard the beautiful voice of the chief's daughter, the cannibal hatched a plan in his thick brain. As the girl bent over to pick up her golden earrings, he sneaked up behind her, scooped her up, and dropped her into his sack.

The chief's daughter pushed and clawed at the inside of the sack, but the cloth was thick and the knot was tight. "It's no use fighting," the cannibal growled in his loud, raspy voice. "I've caught you, and you must obey my orders. If not, I'll eat you right now."

Slinging the sack over his shoulder, the giant cannibal hopped on his one huge foot through the bush until he came to a nearby village. By this time he was very hungry, so he shouted to the villagers, "I have a wonderful bird in this sack! It sings like no other bird you've ever heard. If you give me meat for dinner — some fat and some lean — I'll order my bird to sing for you."

The villagers gladly gave the cannibal a large helping of meat. When he was full, he turned to the sack and ordered, "Sing, my bird!"

The clear, beautiful voice of the chief's daughter carried through the sack and delighted the people of the village. The cannibal was right, they agreed. It was like no other bird they had ever heard. It sounded almost human.

"Can we see your bird?" they asked the cannibal. "We will give you more meat in the morning."

Although the cannibal was very fond of meat, he refused to open his sack. "There are many other villages," he declared. "And they will all give me meat for a song from my wonderful bird." Then he slung the sack over his shoulder and hopped off into the night.

In the meantime, the other girls arrived at their own village. When the chief asked about his daughter, they were ashamed to tell him they had let her go into the bush alone. So they made up a story, saying that she had met her cousins at the pond and decided to go to their village for a visit.

"Ah," said the chief, "what an excellent idea! I'd been thinking of visiting them myself. But I hope she remembers the feast on the day after tomorrow."

The next day, the giant cannibal visited three different villages for breakfast, lunch, and dinner. At each village he ordered his wonderful bird to sing in return for meat—some fat and some lean. All the villagers listened with delight to the clear, beautiful song. But though they begged to see his wonderful bird, the giant cannibal refused to open his sack.

On the third day, the cannibal arrived at the village of the chief's daughter. The great feast was already in progress, and he found a group of boys eating outside the village. "That meat looks delicious!" cried the cannibal. "If you share it with me—some fat and some lean—I'll order my wonderful bird to sing for you."

There was plenty of meat, so the boys gladly shared the fat and the lean with the giant cannibal. When he was finished, he turned to the sack and ordered, "Sing, my bird!"

The clear, beautiful voice of the chief's daughter carried through the cloth and delighted the ears of the boys—or at least most of the boys. One of them was the chief's son, and he thought the voice of the cannibal's bird sounded just like the voice of his sister. He was afraid to ask the cannibal to open the sack, so he sent the monster to his father, saying, "Today we are having a great feast.

49

If you take your bird to the chief, he will give you more meat than you ever dreamed of."

This sounded like an excellent idea to the cannibal, so he slung the sack over his shoulder and hopped into the village. When he found the chief, he exclaimed, "I see you have plenty of meat today! If you give me all I want — some fat and some lean — I'll order my wonderful bird to sing for you. She is like no other bird you've ever heard. I promise you won't be disappointed."

Naturally, the chief was eager to hear such a wonderful bird. So he gave the cannibal all the fat and lean he could eat — which was a lot of meat. When he was finally full, the cannibal turned to his sack and ordered, "Sing, my bird!"

The clear, beautiful voice of the chief's daughter carried through the sack and filled the village with delight. But the chief felt uneasy. The cannibal's wonderful bird sounded just like his daughter. Of course, it couldn't be his daughter, because she was visiting her cousins. But still he wanted to see the bird.

"I will give you a whole ox if you open your sack," the chief offered.

"I would gladly take your ox," the cannibal replied, "but I will never open my sack."

"What if I give you two oxen?" asked the chief.

"Two oxen!" The giant cannibal licked his lips. "Now that would be delicious. But I still won't open my sack."

The chief thought for a moment. Then he made a new offer. "All right. I see that you won't open your sack. But I will give you two oxen if you fetch some water for us. We are very thirsty after all this feasting."

The cannibal rose onto his one huge foot and hopped up and down in excitement. "Now that is an excellent offer!" he shouted. "Just give me a jar to fetch the water, and I'll be back in no time. But you must promise not to touch my sack while I'm gone."

"Of course, I promise," the chief declared. Then he gave the giant cannibal a big water jar with a leaky bottom. "That should keep him busy for a while," he muttered. As soon as the cannibal was out of the village, the chief opened the sack and stared in amazement at his daughter.

"Oh, Father!" she cried. "You've saved me!"

"But I thought you were visiting your cousins," said the chief.

"My cousins? I haven't seen them in months." She told her father the whole story, and he ordered the other girls punished for telling him a lie. Then he put snakes and toads into the giant cannibal's sack and tied the knot tight. When the cannibal returned with the water, his sack sat just where he left it, and the chief's daughter was hidden from sight.

"You gave me a leaky water jar," the cannibal complained. "It took me hours to fill it."

"I'm sorry," replied the chief. "I must have given you the wrong jar by mistake. But here, eat some more meat and let's forget about it. I've killed two oxen just for you."

The giant cannibal ate the meat of two oxen—all the fat and all the lean—until he was full again. Then he slung his sack over his shoulder and hopped out of the village. He kept hopping through the bush until he came to his own house and handed the sack to his wife. "Throw this in the cooking pot," he ordered. "We're going to have a real feast."

While his wife cooked the sack, the giant cannibal invited all the other cannibals in the neighborhood to join him for the feast. "A tasty young girl," he promised. "Absolutely delicious!"

When the other cannibals arrived at his house, he made them wait until they were really hungry. Finally, he pulled the sack out of the cooking pot and opened it before his guests. "Here's a real feast," he announced proudly. "Enjoy!"

But instead of a tasty young girl, they found nothing but disgusting snakes and toads. The other cannibals were so angry and hungry that they killed the giant cannibal and ate him instead.

This story is based on a tale told by the Xhosa people who live in the Republic of South Africa. The tale was included in a collection of African stories published in 1921 by a French poet named Blaise Cendrars. Cendrars did not indicate where he found each story, but he presented them in their earliest published forms, as written down by European missionaries and explorers.

A longer but very similar version of this tale was told by a Xhosa storyteller in 1967 and recorded by folklorist Harold Scheub. Although I have followed the plot and main ideas of Cendrars' version, I've borrowed some details from the more recent version and added dialogue and details of my own to further develop the tale.

The one-legged giant cannibal is a Zim, the favorite villain in stories told by the Xhosa and the neighboring Zulu tribe. According to some stories, a Zim is born with two legs—one sweet and one bitter—but his parents immediately bite off the sweet leg and eat it.

Different versions of this tale are told by other African tribes. In the Swahili story, the girl returns to the seashore for a beautiful shell and is kidnapped by a fairy who places her in a barrel. In the Umbundo version, a young boy is kidnapped by an ogre while picking guavas. But the main idea of all these stories is the same: a young person is kidnapped by a strange being and forced to sing until the kidnapper is outwitted and punished.

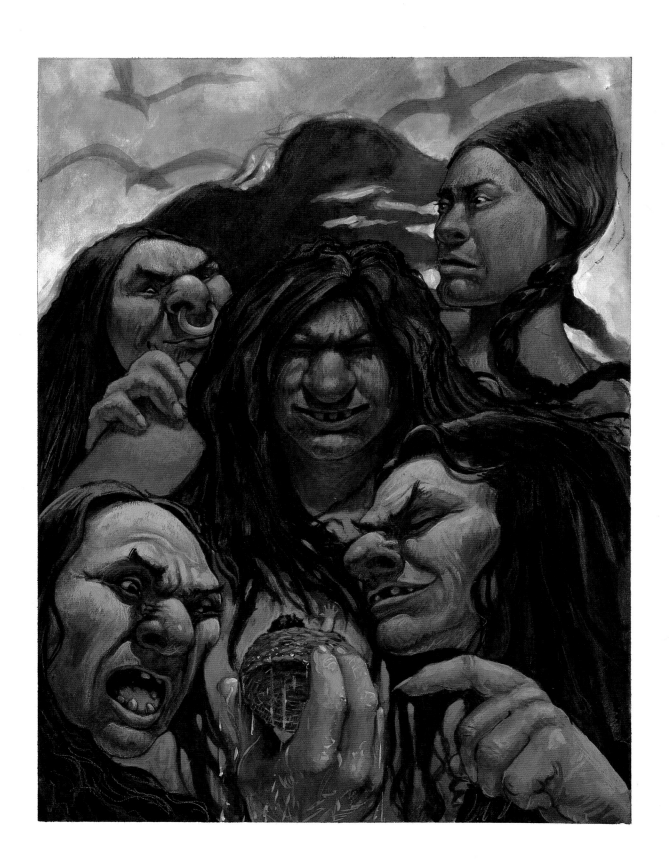

COYOTE AND THE GIANT SISTERS

Pacific Northwest

L ONG AGO, before the world turned inside out, the Animal People lived on the banks of Big River, the one we call the Columbia. The Animal People were not like animals of today—they were bigger and smarter, and they could take off their fur or feathers and look like humans. They talked and made fires and lived in lodges. They hunted for deer in the woods and fished for salmon in Big River.

Then one day the salmon disappeared. Other fish, too. There was nothing but water and rocks in Big River. So the Animal People called a great council to discuss the problem.

Grizzly spoke first, for he was chief. "This is bad," he declared. "Salmon is my favorite food."

"It's worse for me," said Kingfisher. "You can dig for roots and eat meat. Without salmon I will starve."

55

"You should eat deer, like us," suggested the Wolf brothers.

"I can't do that!" cried Kingfisher. "I eat only fish!"

Like white water rushing over rocks, all the Animal People yelled and argued, with fish eaters angry at meat eaters, meat eaters angry at fish eaters, and root eaters angry at everyone.

In the midst of the ruckus, Coyote raised his hand. "Brothers, listen!" he commanded. "Roots are good. Deer is good. Salmon is good. All are good. I like a nice, fat salmon myself. And I know something you don't know."

The Animal People looked at Coyote curiously and waited for what he had to say. Though he made mischief with jokes and tricks, they knew he had great powers — greater than any of them.

"A new people are coming to the earth," Coyote explained. "Human People. And they will need salmon for food."

"What should we do?" asked Grizzly.

Coyote stood before the council fire. "Leave it to me," he said. "I'll float down Big River and find the salmon."

"But how?" asked Kingfisher.

Coyote smiled. "Leave it to me."

Near the water, Coyote gathered strong reeds and made a basket just like a baby's cradle. Then he climbed into the basket and changed himself into a cute little baby. He pushed off from the bank and floated down Big River for many days, until he came to a huge dam of logs and mud built from shore to shore. He couldn't float any farther, so Coyote just bobbed up and down in his cradle and wailed like a baby.

Now five giant sisters lived in that place, and these sisters had built the dam to make a fish trap so they could keep all the salmon for themselves. That afternoon the sisters came out of the forest, where they had been gathering roots. They were about to check their fish trap, when the oldest sister heard a baby crying and noticed the basket floating on Big River.

"Look!" she called. "Someone must have drowned. There's a baby floating all by himself. Let's rescue the poor thing."

"Yes," the second sister agreed. "If it's a boy, we can raise him as our brother."

"He will be a great help to us," the third pointed out.

"He can do all the fishing," the fourth added, "and we can just dry the fish he catches."

"No, wait!" cried the youngest sister. "How do we know it's really a baby? Maybe it's Coyote!"

But the four older sisters paid no attention to the youngest. They waded out into the river and lifted the cradle from the water. Coyote smiled up at them and made sweet, cooing baby sounds.

"Look," said the oldest, "what a cute little baby!"

"It's a boy!" exclaimed the second. "He can be our brother."

"He's awfully small," the third noticed. "Maybe we won't be able to raise him."

"Let's take him home and try," suggested the fourth. And so they took the baby home to their lodge, with the youngest sister following silently behind.

After his long journey down Big River, Coyote was tired and hungry, so when the oldest sister put the tail of an eel in his mouth, he sucked on it just like a baby until he fell asleep. That is why the eel has no tail, for Coyote sucked it all away.

"Look!" cried the second sister as she watched the sucking baby.

"He's old enough to eat. We can raise him to be our brother."

All that night, the giant sisters rocked Coyote's cradle, happy to have a little baby sleeping in their lodge. Even the youngest sister had to admit he was the cutest baby she had ever seen. But the next morning, when the giants went out into the woods to dig for roots, Coyote slipped out of his cradle and changed into the form of a man. He headed straight for the fish trap and found thousands of big pink and silver salmon swimming behind the dam.

"This is food for the Animal People," said Coyote, "and for the Human People to come. I'll dig a canal through the dam and let the salmon up Big River."

Coyote made five wooden diggers and began to dig the canal. All day he dug, until it was time for the sisters to return to their lodge. Then he changed back into a baby and lay waiting for them in the cradle. That night again, he fell asleep sucking on an eel's tail. But the next morning, when the sisters went out to look for roots, Coyote became a man and continued digging the canal.

This went on for four days, with Coyote digging a little farther each day. Finally, on the fifth day, he was almost ready to let the fish out of the trap. But Coyote knew that the work would take him all afternoon, and he might not finish before the sisters came home from the woods. So he made a plan.

Each of the five sisters had a hard horn spoon that she used for eating. They were just spoons for the giants, but they were like big bowls for Coyote. On the morning of the fifth day, after the sisters had left for the woods, Coyote took the five horn spoons and placed them on his head, one on top of the other. Then he went out to dig the canal. He worked hard all day, and he almost finished without the giant sisters catching him.

But just then, out in the woods, the oldest sister broke her digging tool. "There's something wrong at home," she said. "The broken tool is a sign."

"Let's run back to the lodge," suggested the second sister.

"Hurry!" cried the third.

The five giants ran through the woods until they came to their lodge. Everything looked fine on the outside, but when they went inside they found an empty cradle — and no baby.

"We better go check the river," said the youngest. "I told you that baby was really Coyote!"

The sisters picked up the big clubs they used to kill salmon and ran out of the lodge to the river. Sure enough, there was Coyote in the form of a man, digging hard to finish the canal.

"Let's club him!" the giants shouted, running like thunder onto the dam.

Coyote saw the sisters coming at him, but he had the horn spoons on his head, so he kept digging. The oldest sister smashed Coyote over the head with her club and broke the first spoon. But she didn't hurt Coyote at all; he just kept digging. The second smashed him over the head and broke the second spoon. But Coyote kept digging. The third broke the third spoon, and the fourth broke the fourth spoon. But Coyote kept digging and digging. Finally, the youngest sister stood above him and smashed down hard with her club. The last spoon shattered just as Coyote finished the canal, and all the fish swam up Big River.

Coyote raised himself from the dam and spoke in a powerful voice. "It's not right to keep all the salmon for yourselves. The

Animal People need the fish for food, and new people are coming to the earth—Human People who will need the salmon, too. So today I make a new law. You can only go with the fish as they swim up Big River. When the people see you, they will know that the salmon are coming."

At that moment, Coyote changed the five giant sisters into five little birds—the swallows that fly ahead of the salmon to this very day. Then he traveled back up Big River, stopping along the way to make special fishing places for the new people—the Human People—who were coming to the earth.

The story of how Coyote freed the fish is told by many tribes who live along the Columbia River of the Pacific Northwest. This retelling is based on three versions of the story recorded in the first half of the twentieth century — two from the Chinookan-speaking people who live near the Dalles on the lower Columbia, and one from the Salishan-speaking people who live on the upper Columbia in northeastern Washington.

The giant sisters, called Tah-tah Kle-ah, *also appear in other legends of the Pacific Northwest. According to a Shasta legend, after the last creation, two of the sisters were reborn in northern California, where they lived in a big cave and ate Indian children. These two cannibal giants were later destroyed, but no one knows exactly how. However, a third sister drowned and all the owls of the world were created from her eye.*

According to a Yakima legend, two of the Tah-tah Kle-ah *once walked through the Yakima Valley toward the Columbia River, looking for something to eat. Along the way, they fell down and died of starvation, and their remains can still be seen in two great piles of rocks shaped like giants. The Yakima people regard these as sacred places, where they make wishes and leave coins and other offerings.*

(I would like to thank Clifford E. Trafzer of the University of California, Riverside, for calling my attention to the stories of the Tah-tah Kle-ah.*)*

DAVID AND GOLIATH

Ancient Israel

I N THE TIME OF the Prophets, the army of Israel went out to battle the Philistines. The Israelites gathered on a hill in Judah, ten thousand strong, their armor and spears gleaming in the sun. The Philistines gathered on another hill, ten thousand strong, with a dusty valley separating the two armies.

As they prepared for battle, the Philistines sent a giant warrior out into the valley. He stood nine feet, nine inches tall and wore a helmet and armor of solid bronze. His spear was the trunk of an olive tree, and its deadly iron tip weighed more than a yearling lamb.

"Men of Israel!" the giant roared, his voice booming across the dusty valley. "Or should I call you slaves of Saul? I am Goliath, the champion of the Philistines. Send your greatest warrior into the valley. If he kills me, the Philistines will serve the people of Israel. But if I kill him, the Israelites will be our slaves."

Fear rushed through the Israelites as they gazed upon the massive body of Goliath, waiting like death in the valley below. As if they were a single man, the ten thousand soldiers turned to King Saul, who stood in his royal armor surrounded by generals and advisors. Was he not the tallest and strongest of the Israelites? Who better to fight the giant warrior?

Saul hid the fear in his heart and met his soldiers' gaze. "It's not right that the king fight as a common soldier," he said. "I will offer a hundred shekels of gold to any man who has the courage to face the giant."

The Israelites gasped at Saul's words. A hundred shekels of gold would make a man wealthy beyond belief! Yet not a single soldier stepped forward to meet the challenge.

For forty days, morning and evening, Goliath walked into the valley and taunted the soldiers of Israel. King Saul offered the hand of his daughter in marriage along with the golden shekels to any man who was brave enough to fight the Philistine. But still no one accepted the challenge.

Now among Saul's soldiers were three brothers, the oldest sons of a man named Jesse who lived in the town of Bethlehem. Jesse worried about his sons in the army, so he called for his youngest son, David, who was watching his father's sheep in the fields.

"Take this bread and grain to your brothers," Jesse ordered, "and make sure they're all right. And here, take these cream cheeses as a gift for their commanding officer."

The next morning David left his sheep with a fellow shepherd

and set off on the road from Bethlehem to the camp of the Israelites. He arrived just as Goliath stepped into the valley and shouted his challenge to Saul's army. Once again, not a single soldier stepped forward to meet the giant.

David cried out in anger: "Who is this Philistine, who dares to defy the army of Israel—the army of the living God? And what will be done for the man who wipes out this disgrace?"

Just then, David's oldest brother noticed him among the soldiers. "What are you doing here, you young rascal?" he asked. "And who's looking after the sheep? You little pup—you've just come to see the fighting."

"What have I done now?" David asked innocently, looking up at his brother. "I brought you some food from Father. And besides, I just asked a question."

65

Though his brother laughed at him, other soldiers heard David's angry words and reported them to King Saul. Desperate for a champion to fight Goliath, the king sent for the shepherd boy.

As David entered the royal tent, he bowed low to the king and his generals. Then he raised his dark eyes and spoke in a steady voice. "Don't lose heart, sir. I will go and fight the Philistine."

King Saul gazed at the young boy and shook his head. "You're a brave lad," he said, "but how can you fight Goliath? He's twice your size, and he's been a warrior all his life. You are just a shepherd boy."

"That's true," David replied, "but when a lion or a bear tries to carry off one of my father's sheep, I run after it and attack until the sheep is safe. The Lord who protects me from the lions and bears will also protect me from this giant Philistine."

When he heard David's brave words, Saul knew that the Israelites had found their champion. "Go with God," he said. "The nation of Israel depends on you." Then the king dressed the shepherd boy in his own royal helmet and armor and gave him his royal sword to carry into battle.

"Thank you, sir," said David. "You honor me with these gifts. But I can't wear this heavy armor or carry this big sword, because I'm not used to them."

So David took off the king's helmet and armor and laid the royal sword on the ground. Then he picked up his wooden slingshot and found five smooth stones to carry in his shepherd's pouch. With these simple weapons, David walked into the valley to face Goliath.

When the giant warrior saw David coming out to meet him, he roared with mocking laughter that echoed between the hills. "Am

I a dog," he asked, "that you send a small boy with a stick to fight me? Come, you miserable child. I'll feed your flesh to the birds and the beasts."

David stood his ground, bravely eyeing the massive Philistine. "You fight with sword and spear and dagger!" he shouted. "But I fight in the name of the Lord, the living God of Israel. In the eyes of the Lord, your weapons are nothing."

With an angry war cry, Goliath rushed at David, his huge spear in one hand, his razor-edged sword in the other. The valley thundered with the giant's powerful footsteps as David ran forth to meet him. From the hillside, the soldiers of Israel watched sadly, fearing that the brave shepherd boy was about to face his doom.

But David had no fear. As he ran toward Goliath, he reached into his shepherd's pouch and drew out a single, smooth stone. He placed the stone in his slingshot and whirled it above his head — once, twice, three times. Finally, he let the stone fly toward the rushing giant.

Crack! The stone smashed the center of Goliath's forehead, snapping the giant's head back with the force of the blow. For a moment, he tottered like a great tree blown by a powerful wind. Then he fell with a crash, facedown in the dust of the valley.

As the Israelites cheered on the hillside, David walked toward Goliath's body and lifted the Philistine's sword in his two small hands. With a single stroke, the shepherd boy cut off the head of the giant warrior.

The next day, the army of Israel marched in triumph through the streets of Jerusalem. Trumpeters led the procession, followed by heralds carrying the purple banners of the king. Then came ten thousand soldiers with sharp-tipped spears and gleaming armor. Finally, King Saul rode on a donkey in the place of honor. And beside him walked David, the shepherd boy, carrying the head of Goliath in his arms.

The people of Jerusalem welcomed them with tambourines, singing, and dancing. "Saul battled thousands," they sang, "but David battled tens of thousands."

When King Saul heard the words of the song, his heart grew jealous of the brave shepherd boy. But though he tried many tricks to destroy David, all his efforts were in vain. For God had chosen David to be the next king of Israel — the greatest king in the history of the Jewish people.

The story of David and Goliath is told in the Old Testament in Chapter 17 of the First Book of Samuel, written around the sixth century B.C. *According to the Bible, David ruled Israel for forty golden years, from around 1010* B.C. *to 970* B.C. *Although we don't know the details of David's life, an Israeli archaeologist recently discovered a carved stone that provides strong evidence that there really was a great King David.*

Goliath was probably a real Philistine warrior, but his height has been exaggerated. In most versions of the Old Testament, Goliath's height is "six cubits and a span," which would be about nine feet, nine inches. However, in the earliest text, found among the Dead Sea Scrolls, Goliath's height is "four cubits and a span," which would be about six feet, nine inches. This is more believable, and three thousand years ago — when the average person was much shorter than today—a man who was six feet, nine inches tall would have been considered a giant.

Poor Goliath actually gets killed twice in the Bible. In the Second Book of Samuel, Goliath is included in a list of four giant Philistines who were killed by David's warriors when he was king. Biblical scholars believe that this story is an older, more accurate version of the Goliath tale. The story of David killing Goliath when he was just a young shepherd boy was probably created later to honor the great King David.

BIBLIOGRAPHY

JACK AND THE BEANSTALK

The History of Jack and the Bean-Stalk, Printed from the Original Manuscript, Never Before Published. London: B. Tabart, 1807. Reprint, with an introduction by Peter Opie and Ione Opie, eds., comps., in *The Classic Fairy Tales.* Oxford: Oxford University Press, 1974.

The History of Jack and the Beanstalk. c. 1810. Reprint, in *English Fairy Tales: Folklore and Legends.* London: Gibbings and Company, 1902.

Jacobs, Joseph, comp. "Jack and the Beanstalk." 1890. In *English Fairy Tales,* 3d ed., rev., with notes and references. Reprint, New York: Schocken Books, 1967.

KANA THE STRETCHING WONDER

Beckwith, Martha. "The Kana Legend." In *Hawaiian Mythology.* New Haven: Yale University Press, 1940. Reprint, Honolulu: University of Hawaii Press, 1970.

BIBLIOGRAPHY

Summarizes versions from the following sources:

Fornander, Abraham, comp. *Collection of Hawaiian Antiquities and Folk-lore.* Ed. Thomas G. Thrum. Vols. 4, 5, 6. Honolulu: Bernice Pauahi Bishop Museum, 1916.

Rice, William Hyde. "Hawaiian Legends." *Bulletin* 3 (1923): 93–102, 105.

Thrum, Thomas G., ed. *Hawaiian Folk Tales: A Collection of Native Legends.* Chicago: A. C. McClurg & Co., 1907.

Colum, Padraic. "The Story of Kana, the Youth Who Could Stretch Himself Upwards." In *At the Gateways of the Day.* Vol. 1 of *Tales & Legends of Hawaii.* New Haven: Yale University Press, 1924.

———. "The Two Great Brothers: Ni-he-u and Kana." In *Hawaiian Legends.* New Haven: Yale University Press, 1937.

THE GIANT WHO HAD NO HEART

Asbjörnsen, Peter Christen and Jorgen Möe, comps. "The Giant Who Had No Heart in His Body." In *Popular Tales from the Norse.* Trans. G. W. Dasent. London: n.p., 1889 (first edition, 1858). Reprint, in *One Hundred Favorite Folktales.* Comp. Stith Thomson. Bloomington: Indiana University Press, 1968.

———. "The Giant Who Had No Heart." In *Round the Yule Log.* Trans. H. L. Braekstad. Philadelphia: n.p., 1881. Reprint, with an introduction in *Scandinavian Folk and Fairy Tales.* Ed. Claire Booss. New York: Avenel Books, 1984.

THE CYCLOPS

Homer. "New Coasts and Poseidon's Son." Book IX of *The Odyssey.* Trans. Robert Fitzgerald. New York: Doubleday, 1961. Reprint, Garden City, N.Y.: Anchor Books, 1963.

————. "The Cyclops." Book IX of *The Odyssey*. Trans. E. V. Rieu. Harmondsworth, England: Penguin Books, 1946. Reprint, New York: Greenwich House, 1982.

————. Book IX of *The Odyssey of Homer*. Trans. and with an introduction by Richmond Lattimore. New York: Harper & Row, 1965.

————. "The Cicones, The Lotus-Eaters, The Cyclops." Book IX of *The Odyssey of Homer*. Trans. Ennis Rees. New York: Modern Library, 1960.

THE GIANT CANNIBAL AND HIS WONDERFUL BIRD

Cendrars, Blaise. "The Cannibal's Wonderful Bird." In *The African Saga*. Trans. Margery Bianco. New York: Payson & Clarke, 1927.

Ennis, Merlin, comp. and trans. "A Boy Encounters an Ogre." In *Umbundu: Folk-Tales from Angola*. Boston: Beacon Press, 1962.

Parrinder, Geoffrey. "Witches and Monsters." In *African Mythology*. London: Paul Hamlyn, 1967.

Scheub, Harold, comp. and trans. "Mbengu-Sonyangaza's Sister Prepares to Undergo Purification Rites," performed by Nongenile Masithathu Zenani, September 1967; "A Zim Steals a Duiker's Children," performed by unnamed Hlubi woman, November 1967. In *Folktales Told around the World*. Ed. Richard M. Dorson. Chicago: University of Chicago Press, 1975.

COYOTE AND THE GIANT SISTERS

Clark, Ella E., ed. *Indian Legends of the Pacific Northwest*. "The Animal People of Long Ago"; "Why Coyote Changed the Course of the Columbia River," told by Clara Moore, June 1950, 91–95. Berkeley: University of California Press, 1963. Originally published 1953.

Curtis, Edward S. "Coyote Frees the Fish." In *The North American Indian*. Vol. 8. 1911. Reprint, in *Coyote Was Going There: Indian Literature of the Oregon*

Country. Comp. and ed. by Jarold Ramsey. Seattle: University of Washington Press, 1977.

Schuster, Helen Hersh. "Yakima Indian Traditionalism: A Study in Continuity and Change." Ph.D. diss., University of Washington, 1975.

"Speel-Yi and the Five Sisters of the nChe-Wana." Told by An-nee-shiat, May 1918. The L. V. McWhorter Collection, Holland Library, Washington State University, Pullman, Wash.

"Tah Tah Kle-Ah: A Shasta Legend." Told by William Charley, 1918. The L. V. McWhorter Collection, Holland Library, Washington State University, Pullman, Wash.

DAVID AND GOLIATH

Harper's Bible Dictionary. Ed. Paul J. Achtemeier. s.v. "David," "Goliath," "Saul." San Francisco: Harper & Row, 1985.

The Holy Bible from Ancient Eastern Manuscripts. Trans. George M. Lamsa. 1 Sam. 17–18. Philadelphia: A. J. Holman, 1957.

The Interlinear Hebrew-Aramaic Old Testament. Vol. 2 of *The Interlinear Hebrew-Greek-English Bible.* 1 Sam. 17–18. Peabody, Mass.: Hendrickson Publishers, 1985.

The Layman's Parallel Bible. 1 Sam. 17–18. Grand Rapids, Mich.: Zandervan Corp., 1991.

The New English Bible with the Apocrypha. Oxford Study ed. 1 Sam. 8–18; 2 Sam. 21:15–22. New York: Oxford University Press, 1976.

Wilford, John Noble. "Stone Fragment Called Proof of the House of David." New York Times News Service. Reprint, in the *San Diego Union-Tribune* 6 August 1993: sec. A, p. 1.